IF YOUR WEBSITE WAS AN EMPLOYEE WOULD YOU FIRE IT?

ALAN BERG

This edition was printed in 2013 by Left of Center Marketing & Publishing, LLC

IF YOUR WEBSITE WAS AN EMPLOYEE, WOULD YOU FIRE IT?
Second Edition

Visit www.AlanBerg.com

LCCN 2013901342

ISBN
PAPERBACK - 978-0-9889179-0-3
MOBI - 978-0-9889179-2-7
EPUB - 978-0-9889179-1-0

I would like to thank the following for their contributions to this book
Editors: Carole Berg, Jodi Bruskin
Book Design: Ian Berg
Cover Design: Ian Berg

While I have already dedicated my life to her, I want to also dedicate this book to my wife, Carole. You are my conscience, my sounding board and my inspiration.

Table Of Contents

Introduction

Thanks for picking up my book. There's no shortage of things competing for your attention, so before we get started, I want to thank you for spending this time with me.

As a professional speaker and author, I choose my topics for my audience, the people that are kind enough to make the time to listen to, or read, my thoughts. To respect you and your time I ask myself, who are you? What are your goals? What value can I bring to you that will help you achieve your goals? The subject of this book started as a presentation I gave to a varied group of small and medium-sized businesses, at a conference for wedding professionals in Las Vegas. The event producer asked me to prepare an entirely new presentation that would benefit everyone—or at least mostly everyone—who would attend. As I thought about what their goals were and what value I could bring to them, it occurred to me that they should be asking themselves some of the same questions in regard to their marketing, and more specifically, their websites. I knew they would be an audience composed mostly of small business owners whose main services and products were geared towards couples who were planning their weddings. Through my more than 20 years of dealing with businesses like theirs, and through having owned more than one of my own small businesses, I was pretty sure that most of them hadn't approached their website design in a rational, well-planned manner. This wasn't, and isn't, unique to the wedding and event industry, which is why this book isn't focused on a specific industry. The challenges faced by most businesses, when it comes to getting most out of their websites, are more similar than they are different.

At the time, I'd been giving presentations to small businesses about sales, marketing and choosing a better attitude for over 15 years. While I still love to speak about print, direct mail and email marketing, the recent years have brought me more and more opportunities to talk about a realistic approach to websites and social media, one that looks at the usability and functionality.

I would have to say that the turning point at which I began to focus more fully on websites was in 2006, while I was vice president of local sales at The Knot (where I worked for 11 years and at the time, the leading lifestage media company providing wedding planning tips to engaged couples through the Internet, magazines and other media). One of our account executives called me to say that a local videography advertiser had requested to cancel his online ad. Despite having advertised with us for over 10 years, and having the second-highest tracking ratings for page views and click-throughs in his market and category, this videographer was convinced that his ad with us wasn't working.

Follow the trail

The tracking clearly showed that we were getting hundreds of couples to look at his ad and click through to his site, which showed me that his ad was working. So, I followed the trail and looked at his website to see what his prospects were seeing, when they clicked through from his ad. I couldn't believe what I found. This was a wedding videographer, yet there wasn't one photo of a wedding couple - his target audience - anywhere on his site. Oh, there were photos... of him wearing a tuxedo in his office (which is in his house - I'm sure he dresses this way every day). In addition, there was a photo of his wife (and business partner), also in a tuxedo, sitting at her desk, in their house. In the photos, I could see an editing console and a video demo viewing room, with a relatively small television and a dated, flowery sofa to top off the experience.

I was floored. How could any engaged couple be expected to feel as though they had arrived at a professional wedding videographer's site? The navigation was poor, the site looked outdated and, worst of all, my first thought was that he must have made the site himself. Now, don't get me wrong, if you happen to be an expert at your service or product and you also happen to be a professional website designer, then go ahead and make it yourself. It just shouldn't look like you did.

After I got up off the floor, I wrote him a multi-page e-mail detailing, website page by website page, how to address the weaknesses of his site so he could see better results: not just from his ads on our site, but from all sources of web traffic. I gave him specific changes that, from my experience, would increase the conversion of the traffic he was already getting.

Good News, Bad News

Good news: The customer didn't cancel. Bad news: The customer didn't change anything on his site for over a year. And when he did, he hardly addressed any of the things I had suggested.

But something good did come of this encounter: First, I began a quest to help him and the legions of businesses like his, through presentations like "10 Ways Your Website Is Killing Your Business", "5 Reasons Why They Leave Your Website in 5 Seconds", "The One-Page Website" and the presentation that's the basis of this book: "5 things you wish you knew before you made your website and how to fix them now!". The book you're reading is the second edition, thanks to people like you who have given me such wonderful feedback.

So, I want thank the videographer (who will remain anonymous) for being the spark to put down on paper and in my presentations, these critical points about website design and usability. I also want to thank all of the wonderful business owners who I've had the privilege to meet through my live presentations, webinars, website reviews, consulting and through my 20-plus years in sales, advertising and marketing. As I say on my website "We're all a product of our experiences" and that makes you a part of me.

My goal for this book is to help you see what your website can and should be. I want to help you increase the conversion - turning visitors into customers - through a better user experience. These ideas work for almost any website, regardless of what business you're in, no matter what you're offering your visitors. They're just as applicable to an auto mechanic as a wedding photographer. They'll help a doctor improve her website just as they'll help a reception venue. While many of the examples in this book will refer to wedding professionals, as many of the businesses that I work with are seeking out engaged couples, I know that you'll be able to read between the lines and see how to apply these to your business, no matter what you do.

The best part is your limited investment. Money: the majority of these ideas will cost you little or nothing to implement. Time: you'll only have to invest about an hour or two of your time in reading this book. I didn't want to write a textbook. Rather, I want you to discover your site's full potential, and see that it won't take boatloads of cash or time to get there. I also want you to quickly move on to making the changes that will have an impact on your business. Then, I want to hear your feedback so I will know that you're moving your site forward (you can email me at **FiveThings@AlanBerg.com** or post your thoughts at **www.ReviewMyBook.net**. Your success is my success. So are you ready? Let's get you started on your way to a great website.

Chapter One

Moving in the Right Direction: Whether You're Improving Your Current Site or Starting a New One

Do You Have to Start Over?

You've made an important first step by picking up this book. You're acknowledging that your web presence potentially needs improving. For many businesses, a website is one of the first — if not the first — contact they'll have with potential clients... so it's extremely important and very likely the central hub of your marketing and branding today. Adding fresh content can get former visitors to return and it's also one of the foundations of good search engine optimization (SEO), which helps drive new visitors to your site. Will you need to start over from scratch, or simply improve your existing website? By the end of this short book, you'll be in a better position to decide which approach is right for you. If you do decide to start over, you'll learn some easy things that you can do to spruce up your current website while you work on that new one.

If your website was an employee, would you fire It?: Five Things You Wish You Knew Before You Made Your Website (and a few more if you're really counting) will help you give your site's visitors an informative, interactive and interesting experience. Your content will appear more engaging. The action you want them to take will be more clear and accessible.

The five things are actually five questions that you should be asking yourself — whether you're planning a new site, or hoping to improve the one you already have. The questions will sound simple, but the answers will require some thought and introspection on your part. The good news is that you already know the answers: Just be honest with yourself about the types of clients you have, your site's visitors, your business goals and you'll get the best results from this book.

Oh, and don't worry: This is not one of those books that asks you to do a lot of homework to get results. In my experience, while the concepts in such books are interesting, most people I know, myself included, rarely follow through if the homework is too involved. It's not that we don't see the value in it; it's that everyday life and business just get in the way.

Approach Your Website Design Like It's a Conversation Between You and Your Site Visitors

I've had a very successful career as a professional sales person, sales manager and trainer. Most people who know me wouldn't believe that I was a relatively shy child, at least in new situations. Now my wife contends that she can drop me in almost any new situation and I'll come out with some new friends. One of the skills that I've learned, and honed, over the years, is that asking better questions yields better results for both parties: those who are seeking information, and those who are providing it. That's true in social situations as well as in business.

Imagine meeting someone for the first time and asking them, "What do you do?" to which they proceed to drone on and on and on, for 10 minutes straight, seemingly without coming up for air. You wouldn't feel very good about the encounter because it would clearly show their lack of interest in you. Now, let's say instead they give a short answer, then ask, "And what do you do?", and then they stop talking and actually listen intently to your answer. After your reply, they ask, "How did you happen to choose that field?" This back and forth goes on for a while.

Which conversation makes you feel better? The first shows that they're only interested in telling you about themselves. The second one engages you and shows that the other person is interested in hearing about you. Most websites that I see tend to be like the first conversation, if you can even call it a conversation. Those websites are a continuous drone about themselves, from the standpoint of those businesses. The sites don't take into consideration who's visiting or what their needs and goals are. The result is basically a bad resume or brochure for those businesses and their owners.

Read on to find out how you can improve your site and make it into a truly engaging conversation with your prospects.

Chapter Two

Question One: *Who Is Your Site's Audience?*

Sounds simple, doesn't it? Who's going to be visiting your site? You know that answer, or do you? Let's say you're a florist and you provide arrangements for weddings, funerals, bar mitzvahs, quinceañeras, christenings, every day and holidays. Now, who's the audience for your website? Not such a short answer, is it?

Let's make it easier. You're exclusively a wedding floral designer. You don't provide flowers for any other events or occasions. Now, who's the audience for your website? You're probably thinking: "It's engaged couples". But is it ALL engaged couples? Probably not.

Narrowing Down Your Audience

First of all, it's the couples who live in or are getting married in your trading area, not all engaged couples in the United States or the world. That's easy. Next, is it couples with all budgets for their wedding flowers? Again, probably not. What about your style: Does it appeal to all couples in your market? Again, probably not. Even if you have a wide range of services, you're not going to be the right floral designer for all weddings in your market. You don't want all of those weddings. The couples that walk into their town hall for a civil ceremony, carrying a small bouquet of flowers, are probably not your prospects. Assuming they don't buy the flowers from a vending machine at the courthouse, they'll probably buy them from a full service retail florist on their way to the ceremony.

No matter what business you're in you need to determine if you have one definable audience or many potential audiences. You also need to be as specific and honest with yourself as possible. Who are they? What criteria can you use to define them? Can you use age, income, zip code, education, ethnicity and/or style? What are the commonalities among your target prospects? This specificity will not only help you design your site or sites, but it'll also help you focus your marketing on the prospects that are most likely to use your products and services. After all, if you don't know who they are, how are you going to find them and how are they going to find you?

Defining Personas

A persona is a detailed description of the typical client from a particular audience that works with your business. I remember reading a case study about how BestBuy divided the contents of its stores into sections for five distinct personas. It defined each of these five personas as clearly as it could by demographics (including age, sex, income and marital status) and psychographics (the way these customers think and approach purchasing items like those sold at BestBuy). Defining these personas helped BestBuy determine how to organize its stores, which merchandise to make available and how the sales team should interact with the customers who seemed to fit these personas. For example, the needs of a single man in his early thirties who's looking for a high-end television are very different from the needs of a married woman in her thirties, with two small children in tow, who's looking for a major appliance. The motivations of these customers are clearly varied. The way BestBuy's sales representatives talk to them and which product features they promote are different, and are driven by BestBuy's development of those personas.

Your Clients' Personas

Can you create the persona of your typical or ideal customers? We already determined that if you're a florist looking for engaged couples, that doesn't include ALL engaged couples. Can you put that description of your ideal customer into words?

Here's an idea of how this persona description might look for our florist example: This persona is a single woman, currently engaged, college educated with a wedding date 6 to 14 months in the future. She has a household income of $50,000 to $85,000, considers herself a trendsetter, likes a contemporary style with a nod toward classic touches and lives within 35 miles of your business location. And, of course, she hasn't yet booked someone for her wedding flowers.

Now, let's imagine that you're a photographer who's looking for corporate work. You would define the corporation that you're looking for by considering which industries that customer might work in, what type of products/services they might provide, the size of their company, the location of their company, what kinds of photography they use (product imagery, catalog images, events, etc.), the decision maker's role in the company, etc.

The more specific you can be about the persona, the better. If you specialize in doing business with a certain religious or ethnic group, add that to the description of the persona. If you cater to a niche market such as those who like cats, or those having a destination wedding, or the same-sex or second marriage market, add that as well. All of these definitions will not only help you understand your market better, they'll also help you most effectively advertise to them. Since advertising is about buying access to an audience, knowing more clearly which audience you're actually looking for helps you find and target them better.

Your business can, and likely will have more than one audience (and therefore, more than one persona). If you have very distinct lines of business, this is a very useful exercise to help you identify each persona of your business and the marketing that'll be most effective for each of those different personas. Unless the entire population is your market, you should be advertising to each persona separately. It's much more efficient to be laser focused on each type of customer instead of using the shotgun approach and sending your same message to everyone with the hopes of getting some of the right clients to find you. It's not likely that you have the kind of budget needed for large-scale marketing, so defining your business's personas is a great first step.

Remember to Be Honest with Yourself

Define only the customers you're targeting right now. If you want to change whom you market to — whether you're adding an additional line of business or moving your current business in a new direction (e.g., focusing on more upscale clients, a new geographic area or changing your business model altogether) — first make the necessary changes to your business, then figure out how to market to that audience. If you make the marketing changes first, when clients from that new audience speak to, meet with you, or visit your website, they'll discover that your business is not yet the business you're trying to present yourself to be, and you won't make the sale.

For example, if you're a reception site for weddings and other events, and you want to move your business up to a more elegant, upscale audience, you must first make the changes to your physical location (by upgrading your decor, chairs, dishes, restrooms, etc.), next upgrade your menu and products, then you can market your business as an upscale reception site.

If you don't make the upgrades to your building and menus, the prospective couples who are attracted by your new, upscale marketing will show up for their appointments, see that your physical location doesn't look upscale, and they'll leave. Similarly, if you're trying to attract corporate meeting business, but you haven't yet invested in the technology required for meeting facilities, your target audience may be attracted by your marketing, but won't be willing to book your venue until you show that you're ready and able to fulfill their meeting needs. Your marketing has to match everything you offer them. That's why a Mercedes Benz dealership looks and feels different than a Hyundai dealership: Each dealership visually represents the price and class of the cars being sold there and the customers who buy them.

A Note About Advertising

I've often said that one of the basic tenets of advertising is to know who your target audience is and then put yourself in front of as many of them as you can. When you invest in advertising, regardless of what you're selling, you're not buying an ad; you're buying access to that media's audience, and using the ads to attract them to you. So getting your ads in front of the right audience — the one most likely to have interest in your products and services — is a very important aspect of good marketing. First define your target audience; then locate them and the media they use; then decide which type of ads in which to invest.

Chapter Three

Do You Need Additional Sites or Landing Pages?

If you've determined that you have more than one target audience, these questions naturally follow:

1) SHOULD YOU HAVE ONE WEBSITE WITH SEPARATE AREAS FOR EACH AUDIENCE?

You can have one big website with distinct areas for each type of potential client who visits your site. If your audiences are likely to need the other products or services that you provide, having one website will help them with their current needs while informing them of your other services. Make sure that your site's navigation is straight-forward and easy to follow so each audience can quickly find what they need. In my presentation "The One-Page Website" I don't really intend for you to have one page. Rather, I want you to get each user to the one page they most need, as quickly as possible. So make the path very clear.

2) SHOULD YOU HAVE SEPARATE WEBSITES FOR EACH AUDIENCE?

If your audiences are very different, or at least at the time they first find your website their needs are very different (for example, people visiting your site for weddings have very different needs than those visiting for funerals - don't laugh, this is a real example from a dove-release business I know), then having completely separate websites is a good way to show each audience that you understand their needs and have the professional skills to satisfy them. On each website you can have subtle links to your other sites, while keeping your message very focused on the current audience's particular needs. This approach minimizes the distractions for your site visitors and lets you present yourself as a specialist for their current need—as opposed to a generalist or jack-of-all-trades.

3) SHOULD YOU USE SEPARATE LANDING PAGES FOR EACH AUDIENCE?

A landing page is the first page that a particular visitor to your website sees (i.e., where they "land" on your site). It could be a page on your website, or a new page you create that they see before getting to your main site. If you have a landing page, they'll usually see it before arriving at your website's home page. You can have many different landing pages; one for each of the audiences for your business. Landing pages are extremely helpful when you have one, large website for very different audiences. They can help each visitor find the content that's most relevant to them without having to search for it. You can think of landing pages as home pages for each audience.

Let's say you're a videographer, and that you advertise your services on the wedding planning site WeddingWire.com. You know that whoever clicks on your ad from WeddingWire is likely to be a couple that's looking for a wedding videographer. You could develop a specific landing page, where that ad would immediately lead. Then after clicking on your ad, the next page that person would see would acknowledge that:

a) You know this person came from WeddingWire.com
b) You know they're interested in wedding information (as opposed to corporate or other services you offer); and
c) You know they've seen and read at least a little about your business on the ad from which they clicked (reviews, photos, videos, peer endorsements, etc.)

To design a landing page for this scenario, you'd think of everything such a visitor would want to see and do on your site, and then provide clearly labeled links to the areas that provide that information. For example, they'd likely want to see videos of weddings and information about your wedding packages, so your landing page would include links titled "Wedding Video Gallery" and "Wedding Packages," which would lead directly to those areas on your website as well as a few others.

Landing Page for Wedding Photography

Now, let's imagine that you're a wedding photographer. We'll make a list of things an engaged couple might want to do after clicking your online ad at WeddingWire.com. That list could include 1) Seeing more photo galleries (since your ad has a gallery of images), 2) Checking on your availability for her wedding date, 3) Scheduling an appointment, 4) Seeing your prices, and 5) Reading testimonials.

Your landing page can start by welcoming her to your site, thanking her for coming, then asking her, "How can I help you today?". Follow that with a few beautiful pictures of couples on their wedding day, and clearly named links to the things you just determined they're likely to want, including a link to your home page. Make sure your landing page, as with every page on your site, also includes a clear call to action with your contact information. An example of a relevant call to action on this page would be *"For more information, or to arrange an appointment with our wedding specialists, call or email today, 800-555-1212"* (note: Never ask someone to call without ending the sentence with your phone number. Make the word "contact" or "email" a link to your contact page or email. Make it easy for them to take that action.)

At this point, you've provided the prospective couple with a limited number of choices, but they're the most likely choices they'll need, so you've given them a very helpful introduction to your services and made it easy for them to take action.

Landing Page for Corporate Photography

Let's say that as a photographer you also do corporate work. Engaged couples and corporations are different demographics, with different needs, and therefore their landing pages should have different designs and links. Your approach, however, is very much the same. You're still going to thank them for coming and ask, *"How can we help you today?"*, but the links you provide to additional information on your site won't be the same. The images you show on this landing page will also be different than the one for weddings. Instead of showing wedding couples, you'll show samples of your corporate work. You'll use language showing corporate visitors that you understand corporate needs and that you're the right professional who can fulfill those needs. The images and text are different but the concept is the same.

Chapter Four

Give Your Site Visitors Something to Aspire Towards

Advertising Is Aspirational

Most advertising is aspirational: It wants us to aspire to be like the people we see in the ads, who are using a particular product, service or brand. That's why most of the ads you see or hear—whether on television, on radio, in print, online or on billboards—have people in them. The intent of the advertisers is that the people you see and hear are doing things you'd want to see yourself doing: driving a nice car, wearing nice clothing, eating great food and so on. Their goal is make us want to be like the people in their ads.

When our two sons were young, my wife and I always had minivans. They were the perfect vehicle for getting around locally and long distance with our kids. We had room for our children and the many, many things that accompanied them: strollers, bikes, toys and more. When I see the ads for minivans now, with the dual DVD players, seats that fold into the floor (instead of having to be completely removed as did ours) and lots of storage compartments, I can imagine other parents wishing that they were the people in the ads, whose lives look calm and organized, and whose kids were sitting quietly in the car.

Ads Show Us Who We Want to Be

It's no surprise that wedding couples love magazines. The national wedding magazines typically contain over 800 photos of wedding dresses. Virtually all of those images are of very tall, very thin women who are size 0 or 2. When I speak to the bridal gown retailers around the country, they tell me that the typical sample sizes in their stores are 8, 10 or 12. That size discrepancy is a pretty big disconnect between what's in the ad and what the average bride is wearing.

However, what the advertisers are counting on is that the women seeing the ad are going to use their mental "erasers" and replace the face of that size-2 model with their own, while thinking, "If I wear that dress, that's what I'll look like at my wedding". In other words, they'll aspire to be like the model in the ad. This is the basis for all fashion advertising. You rarely see clothing ads without people wearing the clothing. It's really the basis for almost all advertising, regardless of what's being sold: cola, insurance, cars, sunglasses, even water.

Show Your Potential Clients What They Can Aspire Towards

What do you want your potential customers to feel when they interact with your ads? You want them to associate with the people in your ads, and to desire to be just like them. I give a presentation called "Creating an Exceptional Customer Experience" in which I talk about how the customer experience starts before you ever get to speak with them. Your website and marketing are part of the experience.

Remember the concept of persona I talked about earlier in this book? Ask yourself who represents your prototypical customer. What image can you use that will make your prospects want to replace the images of the people in your ad with their own?

It amazes me to see ads for wedding reception venues that are trying to attract wedding couples, yet they only show photos of empty banquet rooms, empty gardens and empty gazebos. Where are the people? A photo of a beautiful view from the balcony of your venue is a nice photo, but it doesn't scream, "Wedding!" Show a wedding couple taking in that beautiful view, and the photo of your venue changes immediately to the photo of a wedding location.

You can apply this same principle to most businesses: Don't just show your product; show people interacting with your product, and make sure they look the way the people you're trying to attract want to see themselves (usually happy and better-off for doing business with you).

Applying the Concept to Service-Based Businesses

What if your business is a service, such as a wedding planner, disk jockey or financial planner? How do you show your clients something to aspire towards? You can show the results of your work.

Wedding planners help couples with the details of their weddings, so show a happy couple with a bouquet or at the ceremony. You can mix-in detail shots of the decorations in your photo galleries with the images of people; very much the way sites such as WeddingWire.com do with their Real Wedding stories.

Disk jockeys set the tone for the party, so show a smiling couple dancing with their guests. If you can get a shot of them dancing that has you, in action, in the background, that's even better, and it'll show off how professionally you present yourself at an event such as theirs.

Architects would show people sitting with them looking at plans, or options and then with the finished product. You can apply this concept to almost any business.

Applying the Concept to Product-Based Businesses

What about people who sell products, such as invitations, flowers or favors (you can apply this concept to whatever you do)? Again, show your prospects what they aspire towards: pictures of pleased looking guests opening elegantly designed invitations, or smiling guests enjoying their fun wedding favors. A neat way to tie in product shots with your target audience is to show a photo of the product, let's say an invitation, and then show a photo of that couple whose wedding it was from. It not only adds a face to the product, it shows that it's from a real wedding and not just a demo.

Note for Product-Based Businesses

Of course, the medium on which your prospect is viewing your photos also makes a big difference (brochure, website, smart-phone, print ad, postcard, etc.). The one constant is that the images have to be high-quality and professional looking. If you own a product-based business and you need to show close-up details for one of your products, offer a way for viewers to zoom in, or else use an inset shot with a close up of the important details. If there's some aspect of a product that makes it unique, but that isn't immediately visible in a photo, show your potential client where to look for it. Don't be subtle here: Tell them exactly what it is that makes your product unique. It will also help your SEO to have as much descriptive text as possible on your site. Don't just have a photo gallery, have captions on the images that tell the story. Ask yourself: "What would I say to someone who is looking at this image if I were with them?" Then answer that in the caption.

Should You Show Yourself in Your Ads?

Now, I can hear some of you saying, *"Alan, I want to show a picture of myself since it's me they're hiring."* Of course they're hiring you, but unless you're a legitimate celebrity, with universal recognition (and not just a celebrity in your own mind), your target audience likely includes many people who don't know you yet. Using a photo of yourself will not attract as many prospects as if you showed a more engaging, aspirational image. They don't want to aspire to be like you, they want to aspire to be like people they can relate to, using your services.

Note: In order to not appear hypocritical here, I do have an image of myself on my homepage, but that's appropriate for a professional speaker's website as I'm the one that will be front and center if you hire me. That's usually not the case for most other businesses. They hire their photographer, caterer, disc jockey, event planner and most service professionals, to be in the background, especially for weddings and events. If you insist on having your image, try using one that has you and your clients. That way they see you and also the aspirational image of someone you can relate to.

I suggest starting with an aspirational image on your home page or landing page, and then you can use a photo gallery elsewhere on your site, and include images of you and your team. Your "About Us" page on your website is a perfect place for that too. A nice touch would be a photo of you with a real, smiling wedding couple, or someone who represents your target audience. It sends the message that they were so happy working with you that they wanted to have their picture taken with you.

Chapter Five

Question 2: *How Will People Get to Your Website?*

This too sounds like an easy question, but is it? There are many, many ways that someone can arrive at your website. **Here are just a few:**

By clicking on an ad you've placed online
By finding and clicking on your listing in a search engine (i.e., unpaid placement through SEO)
By seeing and clicking on your search engine marketing ads (keyword ads you've paid to have placed on search engines)
By typing in your website's address from a print ad
By typing in your website's address from your collateral material: brochures, business cards, mailing pieces, etc.

By clicking on a link in an email that you sent them, or one that was sent for you (a paid email advertisement)

By clicking on your link from another website, perhaps the website of someone in your industry with whom you've traded links, or who refers business to you

By clicking on your link from your blog (if it's not directly a part of your website, which it should be)

By clicking on your link from someone else's blog (perhaps the blog of someone who referenced you because they've used your services, or who works in your industry)

By clicking on your link from a social media site (e.g., Facebook, Twitter, Google+ or LinkedIn)

By clicking on a link from your photo or video content on a site like YouTube, Pinterest, Instagram, Vimeo or Flickr

Consider What Prospects Know About Your Business When They Arrive at Your Site

What I want you to think about here is what each of these visitors knows about your business when they arrive at your site. Someone coming from an online ad or a print ad in a magazine already knows something about your company (what they saw and read in the ad), while someone coming from a search engine may know very little about it. Someone who clicked your link that's provided on another website may only know that you were on the list of recommended *"Invitation Designers"*, but they don't know what types of invitations you create, your price range, location or your personality. When these prospects arrive at your site they'll need to have more information than someone who came from your online ad, who already has an idea of the types of invitations you design. Again, this is where landing pages can be useful in taking each audience from each separate entry path to the next logical step, rather than moving them back a step, or more, to your home page.

Choosing the Right Medium for Your Ads

Good advertising acts as a filter. It filters everyone who sees your ad down to those who are most interested in your product or service.

Choosing the right medium for your ads is part of the filtering process. If you're looking for wedding couples you wouldn't advertise in a men's sports magazine. Even placing the most well-designed wedding ad in that men's sports magazine would be unlikely to yield significant results. When you choose a magazine or website in which to advertise, and you buy your placement based upon the size and quality of the audience who uses that medium, you're using a filter so that only the most promising prospects will see your ads. All media filters a larger audience down to a more targeted one. Then, your ad on that media itself acts as a finer filter, by attracting the right prospects from the already filtered audience: those who need, want and can afford your service.

All clicks are not created equal

When considering which media to use for ads, you must factor in the conversion rate for those media. The conversion rate, in its simplest form, is the number of prospects (i.e., people who see your ad) who contact you and then become customers, compared to the total number of people who saw your ad. You don't just want more people viewing your ads: you want more of the right people — those who want your type of service or product — to view them. For online ads, for example, I have people telling me all the time that they buy their ads based upon the cost per click to their website link. But your cost per click is irrelevant if you don't know how much business you're getting from each click.

When I ask those same people for their revenue per click (how much money they average from each click to their website from an online ad), the room goes silent. They don't know, because they fail to connect the dots from the ad to the actual business it creates.

Advertising is not about the cost; it's about the return on your investment (ROI). If you can get a positive ROI from a particular advertising method, then you should probably do it.

Let's say you're a professional videographer and your average job brings you $3,000. Does it really matter if the average cost per click of an ad is $1, $5, or $50 if every one of those clicks brings you an average of $3,000? Of course not. Now, let's say that one of the websites on which you advertise brings you three times as many clicks as another site, but no more revenue. Your cost per click may be lower, but your bottom line is no richer. So you see, cost per click is not enough information: You need to follow the trail all the way to the sale.

I could write a whole book on conversion and ROI... Hey, that's not a bad idea... stay tuned.

Chapter Six

Tracking Your Website Traffic to Learn Your Visitors' Needs

Nowadays, there are many free resources for "tracking" your website traffic. For example, Google Analytics can show you the number of visitors to your site, where they came from (i.e., did they click a particular ad, your profile on Facebook, or did they click your link on a friend's site?) and even which was the last page they viewed before exiting your site. Website tracking software provides invaluable insight into how your visitors are interacting with your site. If you aren't currently tracking your site's traffic, I would advise you to start as soon as possible.

One caveat about tracking software: don't just install the tracking software, you need to also learn how to read the reports. If you don't know how to interpret the data, you'll end up making important business decisions based upon incomplete, or wrong information. If I sat in the cockpit of an airplane there would be many gauges in front me, providing valuable information... if I were a pilot. Since I'm not a pilot and don't know what I'm looking at, that valuable data becomes almost useless. That's what it's like for you to read a website analytics report without learning what all of that data means to you and your business.

Consider Hiring a Web Master

Your webmaster can help you with reading your tracking reports and setting up tracking, if you don't have it already. Don't have a webmaster? This is yet another reason to hire a professional to make your site. You want your prospects to hire you because you're a professional in your industry. You have the knowledge and experience to best help them. Shouldn't you use the same logic when it comes to your website... which is likely to be your prospect's first impression of your business?

Follow the Bouncing Visitor

One way to gauge the quality of the visitors to your website from different sources is by looking at your bounce rate. What's a bounce rate? Have you ever clicked onto a website, only to find that it wasn't what you were looking for, so you left without visiting any other pages on that site? You left from the same page on which you arrived, so you "bounced" off that site.

On your site's tracking report, look at the bounce rate from each traffic source (i.e., referring site, search term or ad) and type of traffic. The lower the bounce rate for a particular source, the more relevant your site was to them and therefore the more likely it is that visitors from that source will become clients. This still doesn't tell you if those site visitors actually go on to contact or do business with you, but if they leave from the same page on which they enter, you have no shot of getting their business. They're gone.

I had a consulting client tell me that Facebook was their top source for incoming traffic, but when I looked at their Google Analytics report, those Facebook clicks had a 78-percent bounce rate. That meant that only 22 percent of the people who came in from Facebook were sticking around to see more than that one page. According to their analytics, other sources of traffic to the site resulted in fewer total visits, but had much lower bounce rates. For this business Facebook was bringing quantity, but not quality traffic. In addition, this customer wasn't tracking the conversion rates of different media where they had advertised. In other words they knew where their traffic was coming from, but they didn't know if those visitors were becoming customers. They could have done this by asking each client how they'd gotten to their website (while they were still on it, possibly on the contact form), where they found their email or where they got their phone number (when they first email or call). Then they might be able to connect the dots between the website traffic and the sales those visits generated.

Identifying Trends in Your Site's Visitors

Website tracking software is great for spotting trends in your traffic and for seeing which pages get visited the most. One thing you can do is look to see which pages on your site people are coming from to get to your online contact form. Then you'll see which pages have the best conversion rate in getting your visitors to take the action you want, which is likely to contact you (unless you're doing e-commerce, in which case you want them to put things in their cart and check out). Look to see what's on those pages that may not be on the others. Chances are they have a clearer, more obvious, call to action (text and links directing your visitors on specifically what action to take at that point on your site - call, email, come in, etc.).

Going Mobile

Your tracking software can also tell you which browsers your visitors are using (Internet Explorer, Firefox, Safari, Chrome, etc.) and which operating systems (Windows, Mac OS, Linux, Mobile - iOS or Android, etc.). If you start to see that you're getting a lot of visitors using mobile phones or tablet computers to view your website, that's your hint to start considering a mobile version of your site. Before you design the mobile site for them, ask your visitors what they're looking to do on those mobile devices when they get to your site. Their needs on the go are likely to be very different than their needs at home or in their office. You also need to consider the different sizes of mobile screens, from phones to tablets. For example, the iPhone 5 screen is longer than the iPhone 4 screen. Android phones come in different shapes and sizes. Tablets range from the iPad Mini to full-size iPad, to the many flavors of Android tablets, to the Microsoft Surface (and yes, undoubtedly some others will be coming along as well). Designing for these varying screen sizes, shapes and resolutions is an ongoing challenge and subject of much debate. Will iPads ever play Flash graphics? Is it possible to have one mobile site that works well on all devices? How long should you wait to jump into the mobile arena? Taking a realistic approach to these and you site's goals will help you design a mobile site that gives your visitors exactly what they want, without overloading it with unnecessary content.

Can you feel the heat?

Some of my clients use heat-mapping programs (CrazyEgg being a popular one). These systems show you which buttons, pages and links on your site are being clicked on the most. It shows you on an overlay the "hot" areas by color-coding the actions. For instance, if there's a button on your site for "Contact Us" and it's clicked very often, it will appear bright red. In contrast, buttons that aren't used often, or at all, appear blue or black (cold). It's fascinating to see exactly where they're clicking and where they're not. For one of my clients we actually saw an area on a page that was being clicked, that didn't have a button or link. So, we looked to see what link we could add there to take advantage of those clicks. His site's visitors were showing us that they thought there was an action item there... so we gave them one.

Identifying Peak Traffic Periods

Look at the times of day and days of the week during which your site is busiest. WeddingWire.com—one of the busiest wedding websites in the world—is busiest during the week, during the day... while their target audience is at work (Monday being the busiest day). It's no wonder more couples are e-mailing wedding vendors rather than calling: They can't call, or their bosses will bust them for planning their weddings on company time. They can, however, e-mail wedding vendors without getting caught.

This is going to be true of many businesses and industries. If you're selling primarily to a consumer audience, as opposed to business-to-business, and you see that your site is busiest during work hours, don't expect a lot of phone calls during the day. Your prospects probably can't make personal phone calls from work. Check your phone logs as well. Are people calling after your normal business hours? If so, it might be time to reevaluate your "normal" business hours, or invest in a call center or answering service. One of my clients invests $30 per month in an answering service, so his phones are answered by a real person, 24 hours a day. He said it's made a noticeable impact on his business. Instead of hanging up when they get voice mail, they're leaving a message with a real, live person.

Why else do you want to know the busiest days and times for your website? If you're targeting consumers, and you see that most of your traffic is coming in while your prospects are at work, consider removing music or video with sound from your home page that starts to play automatically. The quickest way for visitors to make your music stop is not by clicking that subtle on/off switch; it's by closing their web browser or hitting the BACK button. Unless you're in the music or video business you probably don't need audio or video on your site at all. If you do have audio or video samples let your visitors choose to listen or watch — don't start the sound automatically. That way your visitors can decide to revisit your site outside of work hours or listen with headphones (so no one around them can hear).

Keyword Optimization

I believe that you should first optimize your website for the people who visit, then for the search engines. Why? Regardless of how they get to your site (and earlier we saw how many ways that can be) your site has to read properly. Sites that optimize first for search engines often read like "Rainman" wrote them (Dustin Hoffman's character in the movie of the same name). Keywords are repeated, unnaturally, over and over. That's why I like to read a site's text out loud, so I can literally hear how it sounds. Is it your "voice"? When they get to speak with you, on the phone or in person, does it sound the same as reading your site? If not, then it's not true to your brand.

Look at your site's tracking software to see which keywords people are using when they "find" your site on search engines. Most of my clients are surprised to find that the most common keywords and phrases used to find their site are their name and company name, with variations on both. If they already knew your name then it wasn't SEO that brought them in. They just used the search engine as a directory. SEO is when they use words and phrases including what you do, where you are, etc.

Next, look at the bounce rate for the visitors who come to your site using different keyword searches. The lower the bounce rate for a set of keywords, the more relevant your site is for that particular keyword or phrase. This means that the people who come to your site using that set of keywords are, as a group, more promising potential customers. Why? They were compelled to look at more than just the page they arrived on. There's no magic bounce rate that you're aiming for, just know that lower is almost always better when determining the quality of the traffic.

Remember, not all clicks are created equal, so even a particular set of keywords with a high bounce rate could still be providing a very profitable return for your business. You have to connect the dots and see how much revenue those clicks are bringing in. If few of the people who are coming from those searches are sticking around, but they're making big purchases, then you can certainly live with a high bounce rate. Revenue per click is they key measurement.

The Limitations of Tracking Software

If you're a service business, which most of you reading this surely are, your website tracking software can't tell you if your ads are bringing you any business. Your sales happen offline. My business is a hybrid, with some of my sales happening online (books, DVDs, Audio CDs) and some happening offline (consulting, website review appointments, speaking engagements, etc.). Tracking reports can tell you the number of people who click on a particular link, the total number of visitors, the bounce rate, the number of pages viewed, how visitors move around within your site from page to page and much more. The problem here is that unless you understand how to read these tracking reports and then connect the dots to the offline sales, you're making decisions based upon incomplete information. Your car's speedometer tells you how fast you're going, but not what the speed limit is. The tachometer tells you how fast your engine is turning, but not which gear your car is in or in which direction you're headed. Similarly, you need to gather more information from additional sources to make the right decisions for marketing your business and designing your website. Again, consider asking the people who contact you how they got to your website, how they heard about your business and where they got your email or phone number. This will help you determine the conversion rate for each form of advertising and search keyword.

Knowing how much business you book and your ROI from each source of traffic (e.g., advertising on Google or WeddingWire) will help you make better decisions on where to invest your marketing dollars.

A couple of notes about advertising: While your ROI will likely be different from each source of traffic, you'll want to make sure you're consistently investing in your marketing, during both good times and bad. Don't create your own personal recession by cutting back your marketing when times are good. That's likely what got you busy in the first place. Don't turn off the flow. Many of the most successful businesses ramp up their marketing when they hear others are cutting back. It's the perfect time to increase their market share.

Don't shy away from a particular advertising vehicle because of the number of other advertisers (your competitors). If the audience is large enough there should be plenty of prospects to go around. It makes sense that the magazine with the best readership, or the website with the most visitors, would have the most ads, just as it makes sense that more fisherman would want to fish in the lake with the most fish. As long as there are enough of the right prospects to go around, the number of ads is likely a sign that there's a desirable audience there, too. Choosing not to advertise there is the same as handing market share to your competitors.

Chapter Seven

Why Now?

Did you ever stop to think about why someone visits your website and then contacts you for more information on a particular day and time? I mean, why now? Why not yesterday? Why not tomorrow? Welcome to my world, because this is the kind of stuff I think about. Was it your print advertising? Was it a search engine? Was it an online ad or a link from another website? It's rarely one thing, but there's almost always a trigger that gets a visitor to your site and then to contact you on a particular day and time. This is one of those moments when you need to sit back and think, *"Yeah, why did they go to my site and e-mail me today of all days?"*

Chances are they're in that stage of the buying cycle, so they're ripe for the picking when something triggers them to take action. Just make sure you're on a tree in the orchard in which they're looking. You don't want to be the best piece of fruit in an orchard that few people visit. That means ensuring that the advertising methods you're using are reaching a large number of people in your target audience.

Identifying the Action Triggers

Knowing what the action triggers are will also help your marketing. If you can find a way to trigger them to visit your site and then to make that initial contact, you'll be able to convert more of the right people into new customers. That will give you more control over the business you book. Make sure there are clear, relevant, calls to action on every page of your website. Don't assume your prospects will know or be moved to take action without them. Don't assume they'll call because your phone number is on the bottom of the page. Don't assume they'll email you because you have a Contact Us page. Tell them exactly what you'd like them to do and then make taking that action as easy as possible: *"Call or email us today to find out how amazing your next holiday party can be at The Villas, 212-555-1234"* (with "email" being a link to an email or contact page).

Chapter Eight

You Don't Get a Second Chance to Make a First Impression

Once a potential client starts looking for a particular product of service, they'll spend a period of time looking over all of the available choices. It may be a short or long period depending upon your industry, product or service. The more important the decision for them, the more they'll want to consider all of the options. Make sure you put forward the best first impression or you may not get a second chance.

Get Your Ad Where It Will Be Seen

As they near the decision point, prospects interacting with a media website will look at many of the ads in a category and whittle their choices down to a smaller group. That's why — just as with real estate — location is key. The ads that a potential client sees first often get viewed much more frequently than those that are less visible. Being at the top of the list doesn't mean you're the right choice for each client, but it does highly increase your chances of being seen. And obviously, once you've got good placement, ensure that you've got a great ad that will catch the viewer's attention and get them to continue that attention on to your website.

Why Should They Choose You?

Do you know the purchasing decision timeline for your product or service? I once read that when someone starts going out looking for a car at dealerships, they usually buy within 72 hours. That means that a car dealer and salesperson has to make a very good first impression, or their customer is likely to move on to the next dealership. The customer can buy the exact same car from other dealers, so why should they choose any one in particular? It's likely the same for your business: Prospects can buy your product or service, or something they perceive as similar, at other businesses, so why should they buy from you? That's a question that you'll want to answer right away for your potential clients — whether or not they come right out and ask it.

Lookin' Sharp

Once you get a prospect's attention, you had better put your best foot forward. Use professional, eye-catching photos with beautiful color. For ads, remember: You're trying to catch someone's attention, so make sure you choose the right image for your marketing medium. If the first photo a prospect sees is a small, thumbnail sized photo — as it is on many online ads and all mobile ads—then choose a photo that actually looks good at that size. You may have a signature image that looks great in a full page print ad or on the wall of your office, but does it look good at the size of a postage stamp? Does it stand out among the other postage stamp sized images? Will someone who's never seen it immediately know what it is?

Why am I asking you so many questions? Because only you can find the best answers for your business. My role is to help you find those answers by making you stop and think. I'm just guiding you down the road you've already chosen: the road that leads to better website design and more effective advertising.

Chapter Nine

Question 3: *What Do Your Customers Want to See and Do on Your Website?*

You now know your target audience and that the first place they're likely to go after they hear about you is to your website. But what do they want to see and do once they get there?

Think back to our discussion of how they got to your site in the first place. Where they came from tells you a little about what—if anything—they already know about you. It will also give you a clue as to what they're expecting to find on your site. This is another one of those times when your website tracking software can help you. If you see that visitors are using certain search terms, those terms will tell you what your prospects are looking for when they visit your site.

What Technology Are They Using to Visit Your Site?

What if your tracking software shows you that visitors are using a mobile device to access your site? Think about what it is they want to see on their mobile device. As we previously discussed, find out from your site visitors exactly what it is they're trying to access on your site with their mobile devices. Again, their needs on the go are usually very different than they are at work or at home. This will help you design a mobile site that gives them the most value, and therefore the most connection, to your site. You'll likely find that much of the content on your main website doesn't translate well to the small size of the screen on a mobile device.

One important item that mobile browsing has changed is that it's not good enough to only have your phone number on every page on your site, it should be at the top, in real text, not a graphic. Most smartphones (iPhone, Android, etc.) will recognize the format of the phone number and offer it as a clickable link to call you. If all they needed to do was to get your phone number, think of how much more convenient it would be if they could click once to call you. However, if it's part of a graphic on your site it's not really text, it's a picture, and their phone won't be able to use that to call you.

Continue the Conversation

If your tracking software shows that visitors are coming from a particular online ad, then you want to continue the "conversation" that you started on the ad, which attracted them in the first place. If they're coming in from an e-mail campaign or direct mailing, again, try to continue the conversation that was started in the e-mail or postcard. Did you make a special offer? Does the page on which they "land" repeat the offer? If not, there's a disconnect between the e-mail or postcard and your site. You need to confirm for visitors that they've landed at the right place by ensuring that the branding, colors, fonts and design for your site match your marketing materials, and they repeat the message and offer contained in those materials. Then, add more value and a strong call to action to help your conversion rate.

Too often, I see businesses doing e-mail or direct mail campaigns without making any changes on their sites or creating a landing page. They just direct the prospects to their home page, and then wonder why few people contact them or mention the offer. It's likely that the people who see the marketing offer and then visit the site, don't feel a connection with the marketing material that led them there — and so they never contact you or become customers. If they go to the trouble of visiting your site after seeing your e-mail or direct mail campaigns, they're obviously interested in your company. So turn that interest into a sale by giving them more of what got them to your site in the first place. You'll likely see an increased ROI if you think of your site as an extension of the e-mail or direct mail campaign. Again, just continue the conversation from where your marketing material left off.

And Surveys Say...

The best way to know what your customers want to see and do on your site is simply to ask them. Survey your current and past customers and ask them what it is they'd like to see and do on your website. Be as specific as possible with your questions, and keep them open-ended so you don't influence people's answers. Try not to ask "Yes" or "No" questions, as they provide you with very little information. Instead of asking: *"Do you want to see photo galleries?"*, ask: *"How many photos would you like to see in our online photo gallery?"*, *"What types of photos would you like to see in our photo gallery?"* or even: *"How would you like the photos to be organized?"*.

Chapter Ten

Question 4: *What Do You Want Your Customers to See and Do on Your Website?*

What do you want your prospects to see and do when they get to your site? What's your end goal?

Service Businesses

Most of you reading this likely own, manage or work for a service business. And if that's the case, prospects can't enter their credit card information and make a purchase on your site, so making a sale is not your site's end goal. They have to meet with — or at least speak with you - for you to be able to make that sale. For service businesses, the end goal for your site is getting visitors to take the next step, to contact you, so you can make that sale. Take ownership of that so you can refocus on the right goal.

Product Businesses

If, on the other hand, your main business is to sell products directly through your website, then your end goal is to get prospects to complete the online purchase process. You want them to put items into their cart, then more items and then complete the checkout process, without abandoning their cart. I recently read that the average abandon rate for online shopping carts is 40 percent. Site visitors find products that interest them, put the items into their shopping carts... but they leave the site without completing their purchase (abandoning their cart). Why? Sometimes it's because the checkout process is too cumbersome, too intrusive or intimidating, or just too slow. Have you ever abandoned an online shopping cart? I'll bet you have. Now, can you remember why? Whatever the reason, don't give your site's visitors the same reason for leaving your site.

Where Are You Losing Your Visitors?

This is another place where your tracking software is very helpful: Product-based businesses need to identify where prospects are bailing out from their sites. Which is the last page your prospect visited? At what stage in the checkout process did they abandon their intended purchase? Or, did they leave without putting anything in their cart at all?

This goes for service businesses as well. Obviously you won't have a shopping cart, but from which pages are prospects leaving your site? And how many pages have they seen before they leave? As we've discussed, if they've only seen one page, they've bounced from your site. What if they're viewing five pages and then leaving without contacting you? This is another place that a tracking or heat-mapping program can help you. It will literally show you which parts of your site are being viewed and which are not.

Once you know where they decide to leave your site, look for ways to keep them there or to encourage them see more pages and to contact you. Sometimes all you need is a clearer call to action and easy navigation paths. Maybe — just maybe — they're leaving because you're not asking them to stay, you're not giving them a good reason to stay, or you're not giving them what they want to see.

With this valuable information from your tracking and heat-mapping software, you can improve your navigation menus, calls to action and content to help direct visitors to the things you most want them to see and do. Find the weakest areas and either remove or improve them. As I say in "The One-Page Website" presentation, less is more.

The Value of Good Content

All of this leads us to the next question: Can you defend the content on your site? Why is it there and how does it help move your visitors closer to taking the action you want and, ultimately, becoming customers? That content may be important to you, but you need to find out if it's important to your target audience. Before you begin loading something up on your site, ask yourself if prospects would, or should, care about it. If it's something they should care about, then make sure you present it in such a way that they understand not only what it is, but why it should be important to them. How does it get them closer to their desired end result? This is a really critical point. You need to get your prospects to understand not only what you're trying to tell them, but also how that information will help them achieve their ultimate goal—be it having the perfect wedding, having beautiful photos to help them immortalize their special day, a better running car, or whatever service it is you're providing them — by doing business with you.

And don't assume that just because one of your competitors has something on their site it means their customers want to see it or are even looking at those pages. It also doesn't mean your customers want to see it, even if that other site's customers do. If you're going to imitate, or emulate another site, copy known success, but understand that what works for one company won't necessarily work for yours. And please don't design your site to impress your industry friends. They're not your target audience. Putting something on your site doesn't guarantee anyone will see it or that they'll care. Have a purpose for everything you post on your site.

Satisfying Your Needs and the Needs of Your Clients

The goal is to match up what prospects want to see and do, with what you want them to see and do as seamlessly as possible. That's why having relevant calls to action on every page — even more than once on a page — is so critical. So let's talk about your site's calls to action.

Frequent Calls to Action

As you just read, every page on your site should have a call to action, although the wording can change from page to page. For instance, a photo gallery page on a wedding photographer's or planner's site could say, *"To see more beautiful photos like these, call Debbie today to arrange an appointment: 800-555-1234"*. The testimonial page on almost any site could say, *"Call today to find out how you can become our next satisfied customer: 800-555-1234"*.

Treat each page's calls to action as a separate, relevant invitation: Think about what the visitor is doing on that particular page and what action you want them to take next. You don't know what page they'll be on when they decide to contact you, so assume that it can be any page on your site, even more than once on a page. For instance, the Consulting information page on my website has 5 or 6 calls to action, but each one refers to the service you just read about. So, they're not exactly the same wording. Redundancy is good when it comes to your calls to action and contact information. One of my clients recently launched his new website, with calls to action on every page (unlike his old site which had it only on the contact page). He just wrote me a testimonial that his contact inquiries are up 350% on the new site, as compared to the old site. He also said that he hardly ever got a phone call from his old site, while his new site has produced many phone inquiries, in only a few weeks. I'm sure the new site design is helping, but asking them to contact and call is working.

Chapter Eleven

Are You Talking to Me?

Talk to Your Audience About Them, Not About You

The easiest way to do this is to make sure you're using the words "you" and "your" more than you use "I," "we," "me," "us" or "our." Write as if you're speaking to your prospects in person so they feel your personality coming through. Too many sites are written as if their high school English teacher is looking over their shoulder, rather than as a conversation with the visitor. Addressing your words directly to your visitors will make them feel more connected to your content, and ultimately to you (the way I've tried to write this book for you).

Want to see if your site uses "you" and "your" more than "I", "we", "me" and "us"? Here's a simple exercise: Print out all of the pages on your website (I know it's not environmentally friendly, so please use recycled paper). Then take two highlighters, different colors. Highlight the words "you" and "your" in one color, then "I", "we", "me", "us" (and any similar words) in another color. When you look at the page you'll see, in color, whether you're talking to them, about them, or more about you. Of course you have to say "I" and "we" at times, just don't start most sentences with "We". Put the focus on them. It's very easy to turn many sentences and phrases around. Change: "We have the experience to ensure that your wedding dress will fit you beautifully" to: "Your wedding dress will fit you beautifully through the experience of our caring team." This is one of those easy things you can do to improve your current site, even if you have a brand new site in the works. If you tackle this one page at a time, not the whole site at once, you'll get this done quickly.

Clearly Tell Your Visitors Their Next Step

Give prospects a reason to want more information. Then tell them what you want them to do and make it easy for them to do it. If you want them to call you, tell them to call, tell them why they're calling (for an appointment, brochure, sample DVD, price, etc.) and then give them your phone number, no matter how many times it already appears on that page or your site. Don't make them click again to see your phone number.

If you want your prospects to e-mail you (which has become the more likely first contact these days), it works the same way. Clearly tell them to e-mail you, why they're e-mailing (for an appointment, brochure, sample DVD, price, etc.) and then include a link to your e-mail address or contact form. If you use an e-mail contact form, consider adding the question, "How did you find our website today?" This is the best time to ask. By the time you get to meet with the prospect, they're usually too far removed from the original source to give you an accurate answer to this question. Also notice the wording. I didn't say "How did you hear about us?" That's a different question. If you want to know how they got to your site, that's the question you should be asking.

Make It Personal

If you can personalize the contact request by telling the prospect the name of the person they're calling or e-mailing, your invitation to connect will seem friendlier and more conversational. If the prospect then calls and asks for "Stacy," this will feel much more personal than their asking for "someone" to talk to about a wedding, or whatever their need. Then, when the prospect gets an e-mail reply from "Stacy," it will be confirmation that a real person is taking interest in them.

In my presentation "How to communicate better with prospects via email" I recommend avoiding generic email addresses, such as info@yourcompany.com or sales@yourcompany.com (talk about getting their guard up, you're flagging that a salesperson is going to contact them). Email is a form of communication, so help them communicate with a person by using a person's name as soon in the process as you can. If the leads come in to a shared inbox, consider something more relevant like weddings@yourcompany.com or BetterWebsites@AlanBerg.com (Hey, that's a good one, I think I'll have created that by the time you're reading this book).

Chapter Twelve

The Curse of Knowledge

A concept that comes up over and over again in my work, my personal life and my presentations is the idea that once you know something, it's very hard to go about the task at hand as if you didn't know it. This is called the "Curse of Knowledge", and it's a subject that's been written about many, many times.

But What's Your Address?

So how does this affect your business? I've seen websites with no street address listed, yet they're for retail stores. On a vacation trip in Rhode Island, my wife and I were looking for a natural foods store. We used my iPad to do a Google search, and it came up with one in the next town from where we were staying. I clicked through to the store's site, and it wasn't bad, just a little dated. The pages loaded quickly and listed many of the brands and products that they carried... but where were they located? I searched around the site for their address. It wasn't on their home page. Why, it's not a secret store? It wasn't on their contact page (this was just an e-mail form, by the way, which I can't stand: When prospects click on your contact page, they should see ALL of the ways to contact you, not just an e-mail form, especially if you have a physical store or office, as opposed to a home office. I can hear your heads nodding in agreement). I looked at about five pages until I finally found their location on the "About Us" page. Really, only on the About Us page?

This was a retail store, on a main street: Isn't it a given that a store would have its address on the home page, if not on every page? I would think so, but when I mentioned to the checkout clerk at the store that their address wasn't on their home page, she seemed surprised. She had been to their site many times, but she had never noticed that the address wasn't listed prominently. Why? She already knew the store's address, so she wasn't looking for it. She wasn't thinking like a new customer. In fact, it would be very difficult for her to think like a new customer because she has the Curse of Knowledge.

How Can They Call You If They Don't Have Your Phone Number?

I realize that these days, when you're dealing with a younger audience, particularly Generation Y (also called the Millennials, born between 1980 and 2000), they're becoming less and less likely to pick up the phone and call you (as opposed to e-mailing). That doesn't mean you should take your phone number off your site altogether. Some prospects will want to call you before the sale, while others will want to call after e-mailing or booking you. If you're targeting a wedding audience, very often the couple's mother is helping with the research. Mom is more likely to want to call you than her daughter. Not providing your phone number is ludicrous from a marketing standpoint. What that says to me is that you're not that comfortable with the sales process. A professional sales person's primary goal for marketing is almost always to get a phone call from their prospects. A call is the most effective way to get an appointment and, subsequently, the sale. And don't you want to make the sale?

I've also seen too many websites provide a phone number without the area code. Prospects outside your area may not know what your area code is. With the increasing number of people using cell phones, there are new area codes popping up every year. It costs you nothing to add those three digits, so just do it. If you only list a toll free phone number and no address, thinking you're casting a wider net, you could be losing local customers who don't see you as local. Search engines are also putting local results first in many cases. Not having your area code or address may be preventing you from coming up in relevant searches by your target audience.

I was giving a presentation in Washington DC called "10 Ways Your Website Is Killing Your Business" where, after the presentation, I pull up some of the websites of the attendees (with their permission, of course). It's a great way to add relevance to what we've just spoken about. My host had just finished his new website and his web designer was in the back of the room. He asked me to use his as an example, so I pulled up his site. His web designer was sitting with his arms crossed, with a look that said "Bring it on, web guy!" When his site came up it was nice. Sure, I had some suggestions, but there isn't any site that can't be improved, including mine. I had mentioned in the presentation about having your phone number on the top of every page, in real text (as I have earlier in this book), but I couldn't find his phone number. It wasn't on the top of the pages. It wasn't on the bottom of the pages. It wasn't embedded in relevant places within the text and it wasn't event on the Contact Us page. They had completely left it off the site. How? When you proofread a website, or book for that matter, you check the words that are in front of you. You usually don't check to see what's not there. His web designer's demeanor went from confrontational to embarrassed. He quickly booted up his laptop and added the phone number. All websites are a work in progress.

Don't Let Your Curse of Knowledge Hurt Your Website

Ask yourself how the Curse of Knowledge is affecting what you put on your website. Are you using any abbreviations or acronyms that are common knowledge to you and your industry friends, but not so common to your target audience? For example, a hotel may say, "Submit an RFP" on its wedding page, but that's corporate language meaning "request for proposal," or "BEO" meaning "Banquet Event Order", not the typical language a wedding couple would know or use. Are you assuming that your target audience knows more about you, or your industry, than they actually do? Are you assuming that you know what's important to them instead of asking them what they think is important? It's hard to put yourself in your prospects' shoes, but the better you can learn to do that, the better your return will be.

Chapter Thirteen

Referrals Are Your Biggest Source of New Business... or Are They?

I know that many businesses think referrals are the top reason that someone does business with them, but in this crowded and noisy marketing world in which we live, it's just not that simple.

In fact, we're all being influenced every day by media, online reviews, personal experience and, of course, word of mouth. Each of these holds some sway over our decisions, and some influence us more than others. For example, we view different media sources with varying levels of trust. We trust the referrals from some people more than we do from others. I was doing a webinar on websites and online reviews with WeddingWire and they displayed a stat that said: "72% of consumers trust online reviews as much as personal recommendations". It seems the definition of a referral has changed recently. It's not just the verbal recommendations of family and friends, it's also your extended network of influence.

Therefore, if we get multiple referrals, all pointing us to a different company, each referral does not carry the same weight. This is influenced by who has given the referral as well as the way it was given.

How Is the Referral Delivered and Who's Giving It?

Let's say you ask a neighbor to refer a good plumber. Your neighbor says, "I use Acme Plumbing." Then you ask a different neighbor the same question, and they say, "I love Matt's Plumbing because they're very clean, they show up on time and they always come in at, or under, the price they quoted." These are both referrals, but which one is stronger? That's an easy one. The referrer who provides specific examples of why they use a particular plumber (i.e., the plumber is clean, timely and there are no surprise costs) is more persuasive than the referrer who gives no information about why they use their plumber.

Have you ever stopped to think about this in terms of your business? Some of the people referred to you are getting information as in the first example and some more like the second. What's more, you must also take into account who the referral came from: A referral from an acquaintance at work is not the same as one that a prospect receives from their sister or best friend.

Consider the Whole Picture

Now, let's take things further and look at this in terms of the connected world in which we live. So, add to the referrals that people make for your business the advertising you do and online reviews. If a consumer who was referred to you has an affinity and trust for the magazine, website or trade show where you advertise, they will automatically have a more favorable view of your company. Even if the prospect didn't see your ad, but makes it to your website where they see the phrase, *"As seen on WeddingsOnline.ie"* (or whatever media you use for ads), this will support or even raise the prospect's impression of your business. Throw in some positive comments on a message board or reviews engine, maybe a testimonial or two, and each of these helps drive that referred prospect even closer to you. WeddingWire also said: *"52% say positive reviews make them more likely to use a local business"*.

So Is There a Problem Here?

Not really, unless you're trying to closely track your advertising and marketing. If you wait until you meet with that customer to ask them how they found you, they're usually too far removed from the advertising to be able to honestly indicate if it played a part in their decision. So if you ask them, "How did you hear about us?", they'll likely answer with the name of the person who first told them about your company, even though all of those other exposures—ads, message boards and reviews—also influenced their decision to contact you.

This can, and does, go the other way as well, only you'll never get to talk to those people since they were influenced away from you. You also don't get to talk to the people who have gotten stronger signals and influence that moved them toward another business. Just keep this in mind: Prospects trust the message (i.e., referral) more when they also trust the messenger, so align yourself with the right messengers and don't take referrals for granted: nurture them.

A word, or two, about reviews and testimonials

I've often said that your brand is defined by the words your customers use to describe their experience with you. It doesn't matter what you say you are, in the eyes and hearts of your current and past clients, you are what they've experienced and how they describe that experience. The beauty of our interconnected world is that you get to see what they think by reading their posts and reviews. Best of all, most of that is free!

I have a friend who does market research for a large insurance company. I asked him what it would cost to put together a focus group. You've seen them in the movies and on TV; those rooms with a one-way mirror where the moderator asks the group of 6 to 10 people what they think about a product or topic. He told me it costs around $5,000 for one session. Most businesses I know wouldn't invest that kind of money to hear what 6 to 10 people think about them. Yet every day you can go online and read what people think about you and your company. Sites like Yelp, TripAdvisor, WeddingWire, Amazon and more, allow customers to post their reviews of your products and services.

Don't get mad, get humble

You may not agree with what they're saying, but that doesn't mean their perspective is wrong. It's just different than yours. So, take the emotion out of this and listen to what they're saying. If they say you're hard to get in touch with; make it easier. If they say you're not responsive to requests; find a way to make it better. The larger your company, the more disconnected executives can be from the end consumer. Reviews are a wonderful window into what's really happening on the ground level, where your company connects with its customers. You'll hear great new product ideas. You'll find out who your biggest brand advocates are, and then you can find a way to leverage them to support your brand even more.

Use their words to support what you're saying. If you take a good, hard look at the reviews of your company, products and services, you'll find a goldmine. They say things you don't, or can't. They'll help define your brand so that others will relate better to what you're trying to do and say. Use reviews and testimonials to say things that would sound contrite or pompous if you said them. For instance, on the back of this book I have a quote that says *"Alan is the most brilliant person I know when it comes to teaching internet marketing"*. That's a great quote, but if I was the one say *"I'm the most brilliant person you'll meet when it comes to internet marketing"*, that would sound pretty pompous (and my wife would knock me back down to earth in no time!).

I use testimonials and reviews all over my website. I have them in the sidebar. I have them on every page, but not just any quote, a quote that relates to what you're reading. If you're reading about my speaking engagements or having me come speak for your group, there are quotes from people who have hired me or who have seen me speak. If you're reading about my consulting or website review services, there are quotes from clients who have had those services. If a client says *"I thought I had a great website, that is, until I had Alan review it"* or *"My website conversions are up 30% since working with Alan"*, those are things that I can't say, but carry a lot of weight with potential clients. Putting the person's name, company, photo, city and state, adds credibility to the quote.

Note: I never change a client's quote, however, I will edit it for length when I'm using it on my site or in print. I may take a sentence or two, but I'll always leave the entire quote on my reviews page. The only time I'll actually edit a quote is when the customer asks or to change typos when I use them in my marketing. I understand that devices won't catch homonyms, words that sound the same and are spelled correctly, but they're not the right word. If I'm going to put a quote on my website I'll make sure the spelling is correct.

Use quotes and reviews not only on a Testimonials page, but on every page. When you talk about how good your customer service is, punctuate that with a testimonial, or review, saying how great your customer service is. If you say that you respond quickly to customer inquiries and issues, follow that with a quote from a customer that says essentially the same thing. I use them in printed materials, on my website, on my books, in my email signature... anywhere I want to strengthen a statement. Don't wait for someone to click on a "Testimonials" link to see that page, put them everywhere you can.

Chapter Fourteen

What Information Should You Have on Your Site and How Should You Display It?

Once you've determined what your site visitors want to do and what you want them to do, you need to decide what information should be on your site and how to display it.

The One-Page Website?

You can't just list everything on one page... or can you? If your business is very easy to explain, and it doesn't need a lot of photos or other information, then maybe you can just have one web page. Don't feel that your site has to have a certain number or type of pages just because other sites do. There's no magic number of pages for a website. Too much information (TMI) usually is not better.

For example, if you perform wedding ceremonies, you may be able to have just one, well designed page. It could showcase a couple of nice, professional photos of you performing ceremonies; some concise, descriptive text explaining what you do; perhaps your rates; and a strong call to action. If you feel you need more than that, then you can always add pages later. However, be careful not to get carried away by making your one page so long that visitors have to scroll down continually. Personally, if I see a site where I have to click "page down" more than once, I've lost interest already, and I'm sure you have too.

As I said previously, I don't actually advocate having only one page. Rather, I want you to try to get each visitor the one page that they need most. Make the path to the information that they want so clear and easy that they get there without really thinking about how they got there, rather than getting frustrated searching endlessly for what they want.

If you do have a "Contact" page, make sure that it's complete. As we've discussed previously, when prospects click on your contact page, they should see ALL of the ways to contact you, not just an e-mail form. In addition to your contact form, they should see your address (if it's pertinent to your business), easy directions, including landmarks and a map, your phone number(s) and your hours of operation. Put yourself in the shoes of your prospects. What would you want to find there if you were the customer? Similarly, if you see something you don't like on a site you visit... don't do that on your own site.

Side Note About Writing for the Benefit of SEO

If you work from home and don't want your street address listed, that's okay. Just remember that if you don't list any location information on your site, in real text (not a graphic or Flash) then the search engines don't know where your business is located and where you do business. Local-search is one of the fastest growing categories so be sure you're in the game. Search engines "index" your site by reading the text on pages on your site. This tells them who you are, what you do and where you're located. They take this information and use it to return the most relevant search results when their users perform a search using some of the words that appear on a page on your site. So, even if you don't list your full address be sure to provide your business' general location (city, town or descriptor such as Chicagoland or the Inland Empire). You can also do this by using captions on the photos on your site identifying their location and in your blog posts, writing about the places where you do business and where your customers are coming from. These help to localize you even when you don't list your physical address. I list the name, company, city and state with each the testimonials on my website. I encourage my clients to do the same on their sites, not just with their testimonials, but also with the photos. For instance, a ceremony officiant client lists the first names of the bride and groom with each testimonials, along with their city and state and the name, city and state of their venue.

That allows him to organically list cities and states, without it feeling forced.

Using Navigation Menus Effectively

For the most part, visitors prefer websites whose information is organized into clearly labeled navigation menu items so they can easily choose what to see and do. Then, those menu items should lead to pages with well-organized, concise content. The beautiful thing here is that you get to decide what your site's navigation items are, so you decide what choices your visitors have. Be sure to label the menus clearly. I see too many websites that use non-standard menu titles just for the sake of being different. It's much more important to label your menus in such a way that visitors can easily find what they're looking for. If a prospect doesn't know what they're going to find when they click on a menu item, they often won't bother to click at all. Use the language that they use so your menus appear more intuitive to them.

I remember a photographer telling me that his rates were on his website, yet couples were calling and asking for his prices (which to me was a good thing — They were calling him). Just because something is on your site doesn't mean anyone is seeing it. This is another thing your website's tracking can show you — which pages are being viewed and which are not. Make sure that the items your prospects think are most important are clearly labeled and easy to locate.

If you want to draw your prospects' attention to a non-menu item, you can also use links to get them where you want them to go. However, a text link can very easily get visually overshadowed by graphical elements on that same page. Don't underline any text that's not a link as it will confuse your prospects. Most websites use an underline to draw attention to that word or phrase, so you'll click on it to find out more. Your visitor's attention is going to the things that jump out and scream, "Look at me!" and a text link doesn't usually do that. There are many tasteful ways to direct your visitors to the things you most want them to see and do. A good website designer can help you identify the best ways to do this. However, if you meet with your website designer by looking in the mirror (you made or manage your own site), it's up to you to poll your customers, and potential customers, to see how they perceive your site and its content. Then, use that information to rework your site to improve your conversion (getting your site's visitors to take the action that you want).

Chapter Fifteen

Question 5: *How Often Will They, or Should They, Return to Your Site?*

We've arrived at question number five: How often will—or should—your prospects return to your site? Will they see enough on their first visit to make them take action, or will they have to come back? Will they even want to come back? What are their needs on each visit? I can hear you saying, "Alan, why are you asking me so many questions? Can't you just give me the answers?" Well, I wish I could, but the magic wand store was closed, and their website was terrible—so I abandoned my shopping cart.

How Long Is the Buying Process for Your Prospects?

You have to understand your consumer. Do they buy soon after they start looking, or is there a longer research phase? For instance, brides spend about three months searching for the right wedding gown before they make a purchase. As I've mentioned before, car buyers tend to buy within about three days of when they begin visiting dealerships. How long is the buying process of your best prospects—the ones who eventually make a purchase with you?

When it comes to your prospective clients, design your site for the second and third time they visit, not just the first. You don't navigate through a website the same way the second or third time as you do on the first visit, so don't expect that your prospects will either. What path will they take through your site the first time, the second time, or even after you make the sale? Are those different paths clear? Remember earlier when I said that you control the choices your prospects have because you control the links and navigation menu items? It's up to you to only give them the choices that are necessary. Really ask yourself about the content, links and navigation menus on your site. Why are they there and how do they help your visitors get closer to their goal, and yours?

If your site can track whether someone is a first-time or repeat visitor, it will help you understand the buying process and flow of your site. If you can take it one step further and see which pages they view on the first visit versus subsequent visits, it will help you decide if your menus, text, images and links are directing them to what you want them to see. If you can get your visitors to "sign in," then you can closely follow them through your site to see how they interact with it. Getting them to register and sign-in certainly adds a new dimension to your site, one that you're not likely to take, unless you have a compelling reason why they should register and sign in.

Should You Serve Different Content to Prospects and Customers?

Some websites have separate areas for prospects and customers. These different areas may include forms or documents that site visitors will need at different stages: before, during and after the sale is made. Some business owners, like photographers, have public photo galleries for their prospects, and password-protected galleries for their current customers (where they have to sign-in). The current customers, as well as their friends and family, can access these "gated" areas to see, and buy, photos and prints. Will your customers want or need to come back after they make a purchase? If so, what is it that they'll want to see and do after the sale? Are their needs after the sale so different from their needs before the sale that you need to consider building a separate website for them? Would a different landing page for customers, versus prospects, make them feel more welcomed? Would it show them that you understand that their needs are different now and that you care about fulfilling their current needs? In many cases I would think so.

One thing that may help you decide whether or not you need separate sites or hidden areas is that you don't want to alienate your prospects by locking up too much content. If you have different sites, or website addresses, for post-sale clients, you won't frustrate your pre-sale prospects by showing them a link, and then denying them access because that area is "gated" (password protected). No one likes hitting a dead end or feeling that they're being excluded. Later, after they make a purchase, you can e-mail them a link to "their" area with the relevant content for them in their new role as customer, rather than prospect. You can tell them about the special, private pages, but don't have them hitting a locked "gate" without explaining what's behind it and how they can get access (by becoming a customer).

Plan for the Future

Do you have up-sell opportunities to current customers when they come back to your site? Things they can buy in addition to what they've already purchased? If yes, then knowing that the visitor is a returning customer is very important so that you can suggest other opportunities for them. Again, try to find out how many visits they'll make, and at what point in the sales process they are, so that you can understand their needs during each visit. The more you understand about the buying process, as well as the after-the-sale process, the better you can serve the needs of each group; prospects and customers.

Chapter Sixteen

There Is No Change without Action

How do you feel now? You've gotten through all five things you wish you knew before you made your website. Will you complete the title and fix them now? The definition of futility (or insanity, if you prefer) is doing the same thing, the same way, and expecting a different result. In order to benefit from what you've just learned, you have to decide to take some action.

Don't worry, you don't need to tackle all of this at once. There are easy wins on every website: small changes that you can make, or have made, will have an impact. Making many small changes will ultimately add up to big results. If you've determined that you need a new—or additional—

website, what can you do in the meantime to your existing site? New sites aren't created in a day. Can you tweak some of the wording to be more customer-centric (use "you" and "your" more than "I," "we," "us", and "me")? Can you add a relevant call to action on every page? Just think about what they're reading and seeing and what action you'd want them to take during, or after reading it. Can you link your advertising and marketing to the most appropriate page on your site? Of course you can. These are easy fixes.

Shorten Your To-Do List and Get More Done

I'm going to leave you with a great piece of advice that I got at one of the first National Speakers Association meetings I ever attended, many years ago: Make a list of all the great ideas you now have (this works for almost any project, business and personal), and then prioritize the list in terms of how much impact each item will have on your business, and how quickly you can implement it. If something is a fairly big project (like making an entirely new website), then break it up into smaller pieces (such as researching website design companies, finding domain names — URL's, mapping out which content belongs on that site, etc.) and consider each one a separate task.

Once you have the big list of all of your great ideas, keep the top three things on the list, and then get rid of the rest. You'll be more likely to take action this way. Larger projects that can be broken down into smaller pieces will often appear on your list, so it may take a while to get through all the pieces of a large project, but you'll be making progress instead of just thinking about what you're going to do.

When you complete the three things on your short list, make a new short list. It's very likely that number four on your original list will not be number one on your new list. It may not even be on your new list at all, as that was what was important at the time and may not be important now. After you complete each list of three items, just make a new one. It will feel much more satisfying to cross off one of three items on your list, rather than one of thirty. There's a greater sense of accomplishment and it will motivate you to tackle the other two items on your list.

What Have I Learned Since Publishing The First Edition of This Book?

Where do I begin? I've learned that website usability is a universal principle. It doesn't matter what you do, or what you're selling, it's always people viewing your site, so optimize the experience for them first, before bowing to the ever-fickle SEO gods. If you optimize for SEO first you may get more traffic, but the people that come may leave without contacting your or buying anything.

I've learned that there are so many things that we have

in common when it comes to website usability. I've never met anyone who likes to read a lot of text on a website, other than content that's specifically done as an article or research paper. Even then, shorter is better as it's hard to keep someone's attention for very long.

I've learned that less is more when it comes to websites. Even for SEO, the search engines don't want more content, they want more of the right, keyword-rich content. More photos in your gallery is not necessarily better. There's a limit to how many photos any one person will want to see. It's better to have 12 great photos than 50 mediocre images. You can always tell them to call or email you to see more (which is a great, relevant call to action).

I've learned, through the scores of websites I've seen and reviewed in the past 2 years, that the people who've had me review their websites have the best intentions of their prospects and customers in mind, when they begin the process. Somewhere along the way budgets and conflicting opinions have worked their way in to cloud the end result. Through many small tweaks most websites can see a noticeable improvement in conversion of the traffic they're already getting. Rarely do I tell someone that their only hope is to scrap their current site and start over. That doesn't mean that a new site won't yield them better results. Rather I prefer to improve what you have and let you decide when you're ready to start over. However, if you have the same basic site design you did five years ago, it's time to look into a new site. You may have great content that can be put into a new template to make it shine. I equate that to buying a new wardrobe. If you've been working out and getting yourself into great physical shape, a new wardrobe will help highlight your great "content". I often use that metaphor with my audiences and clients. I'm working on a new website for my services and products, even though my current site is pretty good. If I wait for it to look and feel dated, it's already too late. I'm making a new site before that happens so, hopefully, it will never look, function or feel dated."

Next Stop, Your Improved Website

So, now that we're at the end of the road, I hope you've thought of some things you can do, right away, to improve your site. Have you started your list yet? What actions are you going to take... today? You know that your website is the most likely first stop for your prospects and customers. They may never have the opportunity to talk to you or meet with you if your website isn't doing its job.

Ask yourself this: If your website was an employee, would you retrain it, fire it or give it a raise? It's all up to you now.

Thanks for spending this time with me and best of luck.

From The Author

Who is Alan Berg? If I had to answer this in one sentence I'd say "I'm a Suburban Renaissance Man". I'm a husband, father, son, brother, friend, speaker, author, salesman, marketer, musician, handyman, consultant, teacher and all-around nice guy. I'm passionate about my family and my work. I love being creative and working with my hands as well as my mind. I've worked in sales & marketing for over 25 years, over 20 in wedding media. I spent 11 years at The Knot (at the time the largest, busiest wedding media site in the world), most as Vice President of Sales and Vice President of The Knot Market Intelligence. I'm a professional speaker and proud member of the National Speakers Association, the leading organization for professional speakers.

I revel in the success of others and truly believe that your success will lead to more success for me and for everyone. I believe that when you give first you'll get more than you could have ever asked for in return. I also believe in living for today, while planning for tomorrow. I know that this information can help you, as it has for so many others, and I appreciate you picking up my book. I look forward to hearing how you've implemented these ideas. You can post your thoughts on my site at www.ReviewMyBook.net

Thank you.

About The Author

Alan Berg is fluent in the language of business. He's been in marketing, sales and sales management for over 20 years, working with businesses of all sizes, many in the wedding and event industry. Before striking out on his own as a business consultant, author and professional speaker, he served as Vice President of Sales and The Knot Market Intelligence at The Knot, the leading life stage media company. He now serves as a consultant and Education Guru for WeddingWire, the leading wedding technology company.

He's able to help new businesses, solopreneurs, as well as established players and corporations, understand and achieve their goals. Alan understands business as he's owned several of his own, including publishing two wedding magazines. He understands what it's like to make payroll, do the books, do collections, apply for a loan and manage/hire/fire/train employees. He knows what you're going through and feels your pain.

His varied experience has helped him understand that the needs of wedding businesses are not that different from the needs of all businesses. You all want to find, capture and retain customers. If you're reading this book you want actionable content, not exhaustive homework and that's what you'll get. Alan purposely made this book short so you can get to the action part faster. Get started now on your journey to greater success

If you'd like more information about where Alan's speaking near you, Audio and DVD video content or his consulting and website review services, visit www.AlanBerg.com.

If you're interested in having Alan speak to your group or conference, or do private training for your sales, marketing or management teams, email FiveThings@AlanBerg.com or visit www.AlanBerg.com

*"Just wanted to take a moment and say thanks. Yours was the best seminar that I attended at Wedding MBA. **I get bored listening to most people talk for more than 10 minutes, but you kept it interesting and me engaged.**"*

LANCE MORRIS
Big Show Mobile Entertainment, Spokane, WA

---

*"I recently scheduled a one-hour consultation with Alan and **walked away with four solid new ideas that will improve my company's marketing program almost immediately.**"*

MARC MCINTOSH
Bridal Showcase, Hilton Head, SC

---

*"I attended my first Conference in Clontarf Castle, Dublin on Monday and will really never forget it! **You are an amazing speaker with such passion and motivation.** Catrine and I learned so much and returned to our store today full of enthusiasm and new ideas."*

MARIA & CATRINE,
My Dress, Tipperary, Ireland.

Made in the USA
Charleston, SC
27 February 2013